The Story of Animals

About the Book

Animals are nature, and nature is constantly changing. Some animals adapt to drastic changes in their habitat, while others cannot adapt and become extinct. The most difficult changes that usually face animals are the changes inflicted on nature by man, the dominant animal. Here is a brief and clear illustrated description of the classes of animals — fish, amphibians, birds, and mammals — how they evolved, how they exist, and the hazards they face.

THE WORLD IS NATURE

The Story of Animals

by the Editors of
COUNTRY BEAUTIFUL
and Dorothy Holmes Allen

G. P. Putnam's Sons   New York

in association with Country Beautiful Corporation,
Waukesha, Wisconsin

THE WORLD  IS NATURE

books describe specific facets of our environment. An important contribution of each book is an emphasis on conserving natural resources. Man has wasted much of our environmental assets in the past and now must direct his energies toward maintaining these resources for future uses.

The Story of Soil

The Story of Animals

Copyright © 1973 by Country Beautiful Foundation, Inc.
a wholly owned subsidiary of Flick-Reedy
All rights reserved. Published simultaneously in
Canada by Longman Canada Limited, Toronto
SBN: GB-399-60815-X
SBN: TR-399-20326-5

Library of Congress Catalog Card Number: 70-150257

PRINTED IN THE UNITED STATES OF AMERICA
09212

Contents

Introduction 7

1 Introducing Fish 11

2 Introducing Amphibians 17

3 Introducing Birds 31

4 Introducing Mammals 37

Bibliography 62

Index 63

In memory of
RICHARD who loved nature

Introduction

Everything on earth that has life is either plant or animal. Animals that have a backbone are called vertebrates. Vertebrates include fish, amphibians, reptiles, birds, and mammals. An animal's body shape, structure, and internal mechanism determine where it will live. The shape of the fish's body enables it to move easily in water. Its gills make it possible for it to breathe oxygen that has dissolved in water.

A bird's body is covered with feathers, which provide warmth and protection. Birds have wings, and most have the power of flight. Instead of teeth, they have a "mill," or gizzard, that grinds up the food they eat.

Frogs have strong legs, which they use for jumping, and webbed hind feet for swimming. They have long sticky tongues they can flip out to capture insects for food.

Among the reptiles, the snake crawls on its belly and swallows food whole. The turtle has short legs, which make it slow-moving, and a hard shell which protects it from its enemies.

Most mammals have four legs, usually fairly long, and are swift in movement. Some are herbivores (they eat only plants); some are carnivores (they prey on other animals for food). Every living thing needs other living things to survive. The owl dines on a mouse that eats grain. This relationship is a food chain.

The place where an animal lives is its environment. The environment, or habitat, must meet certain basic requirements of the animal for it to survive. All animals must have food, water, and shelter. These necessities depend on four basic natural factors — air, water, sun, and rock. Without rock, there would be no soil; without soil, sun, air, and water, there would be practically no plant life; without plants, no animal life. Water is essential to all life. Air contains oxygen, which animals need to breathe, and carbon dioxide, which is converted into oxygen by plants for growth. From plant life comes food which helps provide energy to animals. In turn, animals provide food, clothing, recreation, and other values for man. This complex interrelationship between natural elements, plants, and animals in a community is called ecology.

As long as these factors are in balance, everything runs smoothly. In an unbalanced state, something may die. An overpopulated deer herd in a certain area may find sufficient food during spring, summer, and fall, but during deep winter snows there will not be enough food for all and many die a slow painful death of starvation.

Game managers keep a close check on the habitat and deer population. They set hunting regulations — the season and number to be taken — to try to keep the number of deer in relation to what the area will support for a healthy herd.

Some animals such as birds will migrate thousands of miles a year to find food and shelter to meet their needs.

Nature is constantly changing. To complicate matters even more, man is constantly changing land conditions.

When the white man settled this country and began to farm the land, he caused great changes in wildlife populations. To survive, the deer, elk, and bear were forced to move to the mountains and forested areas. The buffalo was not allowed on farmed land or lands used for grazing cattle. These great beasts were killed. There are only a few herds of buffalo left today. These herds are protected by the government.

Some animals cannot continue to live where man builds shopping centers and highways, while other animals are able to share the use of land along with man and thrive. Whether or not an animal survives depends on its ability to adjust to environmental changes that are constantly taking place.

When man can bring about a state of harmony between himself and the land (all natural resources including wildlife), he is practicing conservation. Some vertebrates have become extinct; others are on the critical list of near extinction. Conservation of wildlife is of great importance if future generations are to have a glimpse of an eagle soaring high in the sky, a rabbit zigzagging across a field, a deer with its white flag flying as it leaps into the woods; or for a youth to have the thrill of a fish tugging at the end of a line.

1 Introducing Fish

Fish are mysterious creatures to us. They live underwater where it is hard to see and study them.

Fishing is one of the most popular sports in the United States. People spend billions of dollars trying to outsmart a fish and hook it. Fishing is healthful and relaxing recreation.

Modern fish management is based on an ecological approach. It considers all factors that affect the health of fish populations. Fish are sensitive to changes in their environment. Pollution of water eliminates oxygen that fish need. Deforestation and drainage of land for agriculture or industrial use harm fish habitats. These changes to land may in turn eliminate food and cover, warm the water, cause silt which clogs fish gills and kills plant life.

Fish respond to fish management practices if their needs are known and taken into consideration. Through fish management work, increased food supply, shelter, and less silt help increase fish populations.

Fish

A fish has a backbone and lives in the water. It has fins and breathes by means of gills. Scales usually cover a fish's body. In the water the fish must breathe, move, and find food to live.

Looked at from above, a fish's body is broader near the front end. It is rounded so the fish can move through the water easily. The long, narrow rear portion of the body with the tail acts as a propeller. It pushes the fish forward by pushing backward on the water first on one side and then on the other. Very much as we swim or row a boat, a fish swims.

Looked at from the side, a fish's body is smooth and gracefully oval. This enables the fish to move through water swiftly.

How a Fish Swims

A fish swims in three ways:

1. Fish have a mass of W-shaped muscles reaching from gills to tail. This is the part of the fish we eat. They contract (pull inward) the muscles pushing against the water first on one side and then on the other. This is about the same way skaters push against the ice with each leg.

2. The fins and tail of the fish are used in moving the fish about and in steering. They also help the fish in diving and rising in the water.

3. Fish swim by jet propulsion. Streams of water pass through the gills along the back and out by the tail. However, gills are primarily breathing organs, not swimming devices.

Parts of a Fish

A fish usually has seven fins. They help the fish to keep its balance. Along each side of a fish is a line of scales containing small tubes that are connected to the fish's nervous system. These tubes are important, for they enable the fish to receive vibrations and to detect movements of other animals in the water.

There are no outside ears on fish. Their inner ears receive vibrations through the lateral line and body instead of receiving sound through air-filled cavities as mammals and birds do. Splashing or vibrations set up in the water travel very easily and are sensed by fish.

All fish are cold-blooded in that the temperature of their blood is the same as that of the water in which they live. For this reason fish become sluggish in very cold or very warm water.

Fish are fast swimmers. These figures have been recorded:

	Miles per hour
Trout	23
Pike	20
Bass	12
Perch	10
Carp	7½
Bluegill	¼

Swordfish and other saltwater fish are the most rapid swimmers.

Along the fish's back is the *dorsal* fin. It can be lifted or shut down like a fan. It can also be twisted side to side and is used in steering the fish.

On the front end of the fish are two fins called *pectorals*. These correspond to our arms. Farther back on the fish is a pair of fins called *ventrals*. They correspond to our legs. The tail is a fin. Underneath the fish and in front of the tail is the *anal* fin.

How a Fish Breathes

A fish constantly opens and closes its mouth. The phrase "To drink like a fish" is a misconception. Fish drink very little water. By opening and closing the mouth, the fish sucks water into its throat and forces it out through the gill openings. This is the way a fish breathes. The fish does not use its nose for breathing, but for smelling. The fish cannot make use of air unless it is dissolved in water. The pink fringes found under the gill cover are filled with tiny blood vessels. Through them wastes carried by the bloodstream pass out and oxygen passes in.

The fish's mouth contains numerous taste buds. The water carries in food, but if it is spoiled, the fish very rapidly spits it out. A fish's tongue is not movable. It is very bony or tough. The shape and number and position of teeth in a fish vary according to its food habits. Most fish have fine, sharp teeth, usually short and arranged in pads. Some fish have blunt teeth, which are used for crushing shells. Fish have teeth not only on the jaws, but also on the roof of the mouth, on the tongue, and in the throat. Fish of the minnow family have toothless jaws and have teeth only in the throat.

Fish Eyes

A fish's eyes are wide open even when it sleeps. They have no eyelids. Because their eyeballs are movable, they give the impression that they can wink.

Fish can move each eye independently of the other. One eye can be looking upward, while the other is looking down, or one eye can look forward while the other is looking backward.

By our standards fish are nearsighted. Some fish can see fairly well up to about 50 feet in clear water, but the best vision of most fish doesn't extend much farther than 12 feet.

When a fish looks up at the surface, it sees a circle of light. If the water is clear and the surface is still, a fish can get a view of the outside world. A fish's vision, as it looks out of water, is limited to an angle of about 98 degrees.

The part of a fish's brain that handles vision is not very well developed.

Sense of Smell

The fish's nose is used for smelling. It is probably the most highly developed sense organ of the fish. Pollution may be detected, and the fish may avoid areas where wastes have been released. Blood can be smelled by sharks at surprisingly great distances.

Scales

The fish wears a coat of armor — scales. The scales are covered with a slimy substance called *mucus* which helps the fish glide through the water more easily. Scales overlap like shingles on a roof. The exposed edges are toward the tail. The number of scales a fish has remains the same throughout life. The scale grows as the body grows. The fish records its birthday on the scales in the form of annual rings. Year marks on fish scales are formed when a fish has active growth each spring.

Fish Habitat

All fish are particular about where they live. Probably trout are the most particular about where they live. A trout stream usually has a fall of 10 feet or more per mile. A stream that has a rocky bottom and swift-flowing water is a trout's home. Trout need a lot of oxygen dissolved in water. The colder the water, the greater is its power to dissolve oxygen. In warm water that lacks oxygen trout die. The water temperature trout like best is 50 degrees to 65 degrees Fahrenheit. If the water temperature drops to below 40 degrees Fahrenheit, trout do not eat. Even if they did eat, they could not digest the food. The temperature would be too cold for their digestive juices to function.

When the water temperature falls still lower, the fish will seek shelter. They go to the bottom of the stream or pond and become inactive until the waters become warmer.

Growth

Fish never stop growing throughout their lives if there is enough food to eat. Life in any body of water is a complete interrelationship of plants and animals. There has to be enough food for the fish to eat. Without plants and tiny animals, there can be no fish life.

2 Introducing Amphibians

Frogs, toads, and salamanders belong to a group of animals called amphibians. They are the smallest of the five groups of animals with backbones. Most amphibians are at home on the land or in the water. They get their oxygen supply from dry air or from oxygen dissolved in water.

About 300,000,000 years ago ancestors of amphibians ventured out of the water to spend part of their lives on land. This change was not abrupt but extended over millions of years.

Amphibians have never become completely independent of water. Their jellylike eggs cannot survive in air. They must, therefore, return to swamps and ponds to breed.

Amphibians spend the early part of their lives in water breathing through gills. As they grow, they gradually absorb their gills and move to land.

Amphibians are cold-blooded animals. Their temperatures change with the temperatures around them.

Frogs and Toads

In their development, frogs and toads pass through an aquatic larval stage, when they are known as tadpoles. The tadpole is provided with gills for using oxygen dissolved in water. The tadpole undergoes a change in form.

It absorbs its tail and sprouts front and hind legs. It loses its gills and develops lungs which enable it to breathe dry air and live on land.

Adult frogs and toads choose to live in cool, moist places. In winter, frogs hibernate in mud in ponds. They burrow deep enough to escape freezing.

Hibernation

Warm-blooded animals are equipped with a sort of thermostat and can go about their everyday living through a wide range of temperatures. Cold-blooded creatures have to make adjustments. When the temperature begins to drop, they curl up somewhere and become inactive until spring. This is called *hibernation*. When in hibernation, animals appear dead. Their body temperature is lowered; there is a drop in blood circulation, heart rate, respiration rate, and other vital factors. It is doubtful that any animal in hibernation can be awakened by sound.

In order to hibernate, an animal must be fat. The woodchuck doubles its weight in four months prior to hibernation.

Some animals that hibernate are chipmunks, ground squirrels, groundhogs, bats, and most of the rodents. When the first thin ice appears on the margins of ponds, frogs bury themselves in mud and leaves at the bottom.

The why, where, and how of hibernation still baffle scientists. There is a great deal to be learned regarding the winter sleep of animals.

Skin

Toads are easily distinguished from frogs by the appearance of their skin. Frogs have a smooth skin. Toads

have a number of bumps, or "warts," all over their backs and legs. A toad's "warts" are glands which secrete a fluid somewhat poisonous and irritating to their enemies. The fluid does not cause warts, nor does it affect man.

Shape

Toads are plump, broad, and less streamlined than frogs. They are slower and cannot jump as well.

Tree frogs and tree toads are smaller than other frogs or toads. They have sticky suction cups, or disks, on their toes that enable them to climb trees.

Ears

Frogs have an external ear disk called *tympanum*.

Eyes

Only a thin membrane separates the eyes from the roof of the mouth. The lower lids work like shutters. When the eyes pull in, the shutters (a translucent fold acts like a nictitating membrane that shields the eye from damage and protects them underwater while allowing partial vision) come up and the eyes are closed. When the eyes push out, the shutters come down and the eyes are open.

Eggs

Frogs lay their eggs in jellylike masses. Toads lay long strings of as many as 12,000 eggs.

Food

Frogs and toads may fill their stomachs four times a day. A long sticky tongue attached to the front of the lower jaw can be flipped with lightning speed to capture an insect. It is almost impossible for the human eye to follow this swift movement. In three months one toad may eat almost 10,000 insects. Most of the insects are ones that are injurious to plants. Their diet makes them helpful to crop farmers. Their jaws are horny with minute teeth which are used for biting and holding food rather than chewing it. Frogs and toads eat their food whole and depend on their insides to digest it.

Toads and frogs are food for heron, shrikes, snakes, turtles, raccoons, and other mammals. Since Roman times frogs' hind legs have been served to man as one of the greatest delicacies.

Frogs and toads are used in the laboratory as research animals that help solve basic medical problems. There are 2,600 known species of frogs and toads in the world.

Simply hearing a big bullfrog's deep bass call, "*jug-o-rum, jug-o-rum,*" contributes to our enjoyment during balmy spring weather.

Salamanders

There are about one hundred and thirty-five kinds of salamanders in the United States. Some salamanders are completely water-dwelling. Many do not have lungs. They breathe through their moist skins and die if they become dry. They avoid direct sunlight and are active at night. Animals that are more active at night than they are during the day are called nocturnal animals.

Habitat

Salamanders live in decaying logs, under leaves in woodlands, under rocks, and in moist caves and wells.

Eggs

Salamander eggs are protected by thin membranes, some with jellylike covering. They are laid in water, and the young pass through an aquatic larval stage. They look unlike the adults in color and body proportions. Some have broad tail fins and prominent gills protruding like feathers from the sides of their heads. The time they spend in this stage varies with the species.

Shape

Salamanders have tails. They never have more than four toes on their front feet. Unlike frogs and toads, salamanders are not vocal.

Food

Salamanders feed mainly on living animals, including insects, worms, slugs, and other creatures.

There are many gaps to be filled in in man's knowledge of salamanders' habits and distribution.

Reptiles

Nearly 250,000,000 years ago reptiles took over the land and flourished for some 120,000,000 years. The mightiest and most terrible dinosaur of all was *Tyrannosaurus* (tye-ran-o-saw-rus) *rex*, whose name means "king of the tyrant lizards." *Tyrannosaurus rex*, the largest land meat-eating animal that ever lived, was 50 feet long and about 20 feet high. The last dinosaurs disappeared from earth nearly 70,000,000 years ago. Why did they disappear? After more than one hundred years of study, scientists still don't know why the dinosaurs died out. We know that dinosaurs existed because their story has been preserved in rocks. By studying remains, called *fossils*, scientists can tell what an animal or plant looked like.

Reptiles developed from amphibians, who were the first ruling land animals. Gradually, over millions of years, the descendants of some of the amphibians changed and they lived on land all the time. These "changed" amphibians were the first reptiles. Just how these changes took place, or why, is a mystery of science that no one has solved.

One important change was in eggs. An amphibian's eggs are laid in water in jellylike masses, and they do not have shells. When they hatch, they do not look like the adult parent but more like a fish. Reptile eggs are laid on land. When they hatch, the young are small models of their parents. They have lungs and breathe air. Their skins are dry and scaly. All young are able to care for themselves very soon after birth.

Turtles, lizards, snakes, crocodiles, and alligators were also early reptiles and have come down through the ages almost unchanged.

During hibernation reptiles require no food and little oxygen.

Reptiles are beneficial to man because they feed on rodents and insects that destroy crops.

Turtles

Turtles today are not very different from turtles that lived 150,000,000 years ago. These reptiles have an unusual skeleton. The turtle's skeleton is outside its body, in the form of a top and bottom shell. The shell of a box turtle five inches long can readily support the weight of a man. The shell of the turtle protects its back and underside. When danger threatens, the turtle pulls its head, feet, and tail inside the shell. The shell serves as a fortress against its enemies — skunks, raccoons, and other mammals. Snakes and birds devour millions of the round, soft-shelled turtle eggs and young every year.

Turtles are very slow-moving animals. Their normal pace is one mile in nine and a half hours. They have keen eyesight but cannot hear.

Turtles spend the winter buried in soft leafmold, well below the frost line. During hibernation they require no food and little oxygen.

Turtles have no teeth. They have a horny bill, with which they can tear plant and animal food. They dine on insects, earthworms, grubs, shellfish, fish, and some plants. They are both beneficial and detrimental to man. They act as disposal units feeding on dead fish in ponds and lakes. They are harmful in that they destroy fish, ducks, and garden vegetables.

There are about 250 kinds of turtles inhabiting the earth. Turtles may live longer than any vertebrate. There is a record of one known to have lived one hundred and fifty-two years.

Lizards

There are more than 2,500 kinds of lizards known, and they vary more widely in size, shape, color, and habit than any of the other groups of reptiles. In size, they extend from tiny forms only a few inches in length to large creatures which may extend 10 feet in length.

Some lizards are blind and limbless and burrow in the ground; some are long-legged tree dwellers, with excellent vision; others are active creatures that run swiftly on their hind legs.

Some are smooth-skinned, while others are spiny, horned lizards. The variety of size and form of lizards represents adaptations that have been made by the animal over the years until we find it existing in the habitat it does today.

One of the strangest lizards is the shiny glass snake. It may be two or more feet long and is legless. Unlike snakes, it has ear openings and movable eyelids.

Lizards may be found in forests and in deserts. Most are found near tropical areas because they are dependent upon that kind of environment as a source of heat for their bodies.

Many lizards have the ability to lose part of their tails. When an enemy grabs a lizard by the tail, the tail may detach from the rest of the body and the lizard escapes. The lizard can grow a new tail.

Most lizards lay eggs under the soil or in rotting logs. Some female lizards retain the eggs within their bodies until the young are hatched. The short-horned lizard and certain spiny lizards give birth to living young. The young emerge as small replicas of the parents.

Lizards feed on insects, spiders, and land snails. Some are mostly plant-eaters.

Crocodile and Alligator

Probably the most feared and hated animals in the world today are the largest reptiles — the crocodiles and alligators.

The differences between the crocodile and alligator are many. The most obvious one is that with jaws closed, the crocodile's long fourth tooth on each side of the lower jaw can be seen. If the crocodile loses one of these teeth, another quickly grows in its place. When an alligator's jaws are closed, no teeth are visible.

The American crocodile is smaller, thinner, and more agile than the alligator. Its snout is pointed and narrower. The alligator prefers freshwater. The crocodile prefers salt marshes and will even swim out into the ocean.

Both reptiles have two deadly weapons: viselike jaws and powerful tails. A sidewise blow of the tail can knock down the largest deer and break its legs.

Like a submarine, these reptiles have a "periscope" (elevated eyes) and a "snorkel" breathing tube (nostrils). With their bodies submerged, they become almost invisible except for the eyes peeping just above the water. Like a submarine, they have a marvelous system of valves that automatically close to protect the nostrils, ears, and throat when the animal dives under water. They have amazing sight underwater even at night. Dividing their time between land and water, they are equally at home on both.

Except for a few small lizards, the crocodiles and alligators are the only reptiles with a true voice. They have a loud eerie roar which sounds somewhat like distant thunder.

The female lays eggs in a nest near the water's edge in sun-warmed sand or an assortment of grasses, muds, twigs, and reeds. The eggs are covered with approximately one foot of nest materials. In about two months the eggs hatch. The babies cannot dig their way out of the nest and start calling for help. At the first "SOS" peep the mother begins to dig away the sand. A baby at birth is about eleven inches long and weighs two ounces. The young run to the nearest water for shelter. Storks and cranes find that the young are even tastier than the eggs. The mother also protects the young from raccoons, opossums, turtles, hawks, and other animals.

The young eat crabs, spiders, insects, crayfish, shrimp, and just anything they can find. Adult alligators and crocodiles will eat anything that walks, swims, crawls, or flies, if they can catch them and tear them into small enough pieces to swallow. Their digestive juices are so strong that they dissolve even iron spearheads.

They do not seem to need a great deal of food. In captivity, they will live on less than a pound of meat a day.

Alligators and crocodiles never stop growing as long as they live. Their lifespan may be a hundred years or more.

Alligator skins bring a price of $50 to $70. A portion of a high-quality belly-skin tanned and made into a handbag may bring nearly $300. Such prices lure men into wholesale shooting of the animal. The population of these reptiles will dwindle quickly under such pressure. Man has drained so many of their marshes that their future doesn't look too promising. Crocodiles and alligators may soon become extinct.

Snakes

Snakes are our best-known reptiles. Their bodies are clothed with a scaly skin that is dry and feels much like soft leather. If you look down at a snake, you might think it has a short head followed by a long, long tail. A snake also has a body. When a snake is lying on its back, you can see where the body ends and the tail begins. The scales on the belly are not like those on its back. Instead of being small and diamond-shaped, they are wide, thin stripes going crosswise. On poisonous snakes the plates on the underside of the tail are arranged in a single row; on nonpoisonous snakes the scales are in a double row.

The belly scales make it possible for a snake to glide across the ground. Each long strip across the reptile's belly can move. When the snake lowers these scales, the scales act like little paddles pushing against the ground. They move either the soil back or the snake forward. If the soil is firm, the snake glides ahead.

A snake may shed its skin one or more times a year. The skin will first crack around the mouth. Slowly the snake will inch out of its old covering. The skin turns inside out as the animal gently moves forward on the ground. The old skin is gray and lifeless. The new coat shines brightly.

The number of segments on a rattlesnake's tail represents the number of times it has shed its skin, not its age. Older rattles are very often worn or broken off. The segments fit together loosely, and when a snake vibrates its tail, they rub together, producing a buzzing sound.

A snake's sense organs are very different from ours. It

has two organs with which it can smell and may have a very special sense organ which tells the temperature of nearby objects. A snake can tell whether an animal is warm or cold-blooded, how far away it is, and in what direction. A snake may use its nostrils to get scents from the air. It also gets scents from the long, forked tongue which flicks in and out of its mouth. In its mouth are sensitive cells which can distinguish tastes or smells.

Snakes do not have external ears. Their entire body picks up vibrations through the ground.

The eyes of snakes have no movable eyelids. The eyes are protected by transparent coverings. These coverings are removed each time the snake sheds its skin. Snakes are believed to be nearsighted. They can see remarkably well at close distances but less keen at longer range.

During the warmer months snakes are active. Most are nocturnal and do their prowling at night. They can become quickly chilled, and hibernate during the winter beneath big logs, in rock crevices, or other suitable spots. Rattlers, copperheads, and black snakes congregate in dens.

The racers, king, milk, bull, rat, and ringneck snakes lay eggs among rotting logs or stumps in piles of leaves or manure. The eggs are generally elongated, plain white, cream, or pale yellow in color. The shells are parchmentlike or rubbery. The young of rattlers, copperheads, cottonmouths, water, garter, and brown snakes are born alive. Actually all snakes come from eggs, but in some species the eggs are retained inside the mother until hatching time. The young, instead of being inside shells, are covered with a thin membrane.

The mother snake gives the young no care after they are born.

The snake eats in an amazing way. It can actually eat food larger than the diameter of its own head. The lower jaws are hinged and joined at the chin by an elastic tissue. Each lower jaw is attached to the corresponding upper jaw in such a way as to permit it to move freely and open widely. The teeth are shaped like curved needles, all pointing inward. All food must be swallowed whole, for the snake does not have the kind of teeth to tear or bite food into pieces. The stomach and intestinal juices are powerful enough to dissolve even bones.

Different kinds of snakes use different methods of getting food. Garter snakes simply seize a frog or fish and swallow it as it struggles to escape. Corn and king snakes throw a coil or two of their bodies around a bird or rodent and squeeze it tightly, strangling it. Poisonous snakes have sharp, hollow fangs and inject a deadly venom that kills in a matter of seconds. The poison itself is a liquid, clear or slightly cloudy and yellowish in color. Rattlesnakes, copperheads, cottonmouths, and coral snakes can be found in the United States.

Snakes have had an important place in the world ever since their first appearance some 200,000,000 years ago. Snakes are the most interesting of all wildlife and are among man's best friends. They feed only on animal food and prefer living prey which they kill themselves.

Many snakes eat large quantities of rats and mice, ground squirrels, and gophers which destroy large quantities of grain. The value of an average snake to a farmer is estimated to be somewhere between $50 and $75.

In one average meal a snake will eat 40 percent of its own weight in food. This is equivalent to a 200-pound man eating 80 pounds of food at one meal.

Snakes are faced with possible extinction because of the rapid depletion of their natural habitat by urban expansion, new highway building, and a great increase in campsites and summer cottages. Some could be destroyed by indiscriminate use of pesticides in agriculture.

Modern agriculture has also greatly reduced snake populations by drainage of marshes and wet grounds, removal of woodlands, and intensive cultivation which has wiped out most of their natural prey. Many snakes are killed by mowers or reapers.

3   Introducing Birds

Our land would be less beautiful without birds. Many people like to spend hours watching songbirds. They build feeding stations and bird boxes and put them out in their yards to attract the birds.

Many men like to hunt quail, pheasants, grouse, and turkey. Others like to hunt waterfowl — ducks and geese. Hunting laws are one way of managing birds. They may be hunted only at certain times of the year, and only so many may be taken.

Birds help us in many ways. They eat vast quantities of insects and weed seeds. Young birds eat their own weight in food every day. The majority of wild birds are very beneficial to farmers.

Many birds have both winter and summer homes. The route between the homes is often long and difficult. The Arctic tern may fly from northern North America 11,000 miles to the Antarctic and back again in a year. Migration is a good way for birds to eat the year-round.

Waterfowl are perhaps our best-known migrators. We call the paths they take *waterfowl flyways*. Wildlife officials band these birds so they can study their movements and find out more about them.

Birds of all kinds are a great natural resource to be appreciated for their good. They are a very necessary part of our environment.

Birds

A bird is a warm-blooded animal with a backbone. Birds are different from other animals. They have wings and are covered with feathers. Because of their ability to fly, birds are probably the most active animals we know. Birds need energy to fly. To get this continuous supply of energy, they must digest their food rapidly. Birds get most of their warmth from the "burning" of food they eat. They are warm even when the weather is very cold. They hold their body heat by lifting up, or "fluffing," the feathers. This allows greater insulation space of a layer of air between the feather and skin. They also increase their body heat by using their muscles through shivering.

On the bird's back at the base of the tail feathers is an oil gland. The oil gland contains a mixture of fatty acid, fat, and wax. The bird squeezes the gland with its beak to get the oil and rubs its beak over the surface of its feathers to waterpoof them.

Feathers

The bird's large feathers are attached to the bones of the wings. Those attached to the bones which correspond to hands are known as *primaries*. Those attached to bones which correspond to the forearms are called *secondaries*.

Beaks

The bird uses its horny and sharp beak as a pair of nippers, a pick to strike into the ground or tree to get seeds or insects. The beak is used for fighting, building nests, and turning over eggs. The form of the bill usually tells the food habits of the bird.

Most ducks, geese, and swans have wide scooplike bills to "shovel in" food found underwater. The water is forced out sievelike edges of the bill while food is retained.

Fish-eating merganser ducks have narrow bills with sharp teethlike edges which are an aid in hanging onto a slippery fish. Shore birds usually have rather long bills with which they probe for food.

Tongue

A bird's tongue is thick and horny. It contains bones and is attached to the floor of the mouth. Birds' tongues are adapted to particular methods of getting food. The woodpecker has a horny-tipped tongue covered with barbs. The muscle tongue is strong and can be forced into a chiseled hole. A large pair of glands in the floor of the mouth coats the tongue with a sticky fluid which captures the insect under the bark.

The sapsucker's brushlike tongue fills with sap as a paintbrush fills with paint. It serves as a tiny broom to sweep in insects attracted to flowing sap of a tree.

Ducks have a very thick flesh tongue that works with their bill to strain food materials from water and diluted mud.

Some Internal Organs

In all birds the esophagus serves as a temporary reservoir for food. In geese, it may be so greatly filled as to make the neck bulge. Some birds, such as pigeons and doves, have a crop. This is primarily a place for food storage. This food can be regurgitated (thrown up) into the mouths of young birds.

The first birds on earth had teeth, but the birds of today do not. Instead of teeth, birds have a muscular gizzard. They swallow small pebbles. Digestion processes are very rapid and perfect. Food swallowed whole is softened by juices from the stomach and passes on to the

"mill" (gizzard) where small pieces of gravel help to grind up the food.

Anything that cannot be digested, such as feathers, fur, bones, animal shells, etc., the gizzard rejects, and these are spit out in spindle-shaped wads called *pellets*.

Body

The bird's streamlined body helps in flying. Wings are used in propulsion. The tail and wings are used for steering. The tail and body are for gliding or soaring. Long narrow wings are adapted for soaring and short wings for bursts of speed.

The bird's skeleton is delicate but strong. Many bones contain air cavities. Their necks are very flexible. The vertebrae in the neck are saddle-shaped and allow the head to move freely. A bird can turn its head almost completely around.

Wing muscles are attached to a *furcula*, or wishbone. The movement of the wings in flight is chiefly controlled by the muscles of the breast. Besides lungs, birds have tiny air sacs in their bodies. These sacs act like little hot-air balloons that help them to fly.

Birds do not get out of breath. The faster the wing moves, the faster the bird breathes. Breathing out takes place with each upstroke of the wing.

Legs and Feet

A bird can perch on a branch and go to sleep without falling off even when the wind is very strong. The bird is actually "locked" on the branch. When a bird perches and relaxes, its body slumps down on the leg muscle and tendon. This causes the toes to flex and grasp support.

A bird also uses its feet for running, climbing, and arranging nest material. Some birds use their feet for handling food and for fighting. Quail, turkey, and other ground birds have stout feet for scratching in the earth. Webs between toes are found in most birds that swim.

Vision

A bird can see extremely well. A bird's eyes are the largest structures of the head and often weigh more than the brain. If human eyes were proportionately as large, each eye would weigh approximately five pounds. Because the eyes are placed at the side of the head, the bird looks first with one eye and then with the other to be sure it sees correctly. A bird will often cock its head to examine an object with both eyes. However, birds can peer straight ahead at an object with both eyes.

An extra transparent eyelid acts as a goggle to keep the eye clean, reduce glare, and prevent excessive watering when the bird is flying through the air. A bird can adjust its eyes for either near or far vision.

Bobwhite (Quail)

The bobwhite quail is a bird that has benefited by man's activities. Totally beneficial to man over its wide range, the quail is a highly prized dweller of our hedgerows, wood margins, and brushy fields.

The species was not overly abundant when Indians roamed the country. White men were responsible for the increased number of the quail. During those early days of mule-drawn plows, rail fences, and crude methods of farming, the bobwhite increased in the weedy fields and overgrown fencerows. For centuries, the species has lived with its natural enemies and survived. Things are in balance. It is when the environment in which they live is ruined, or when they are hunted too greatly by man, that quail disappear.

4 Introducing Mammals

Every year mammals provide furs worth millions of dollars. To a woman, fur is a luxury item for her wardrobe. A fur wrap may cost hundreds or even thousands of dollars depending on the mammal it comes from and the workmanship that goes into making the pelts into a beautiful wrap.

Men who like the sport of hunting game mammals spend vast sums of money on guns, ammunition, camping equipment, and travel.

Mammals have a great influence upon one another, upon the land on which they live, and indirectly upon humans. Tunnels of shrews and mice in the leafy litter of a forest floor catch and help slow down the runoff from seasonal rains and melting snows. The increase of water stored underground helps prevent flooding of streams and rivers, and this in turn affects the fisherman and his catch.

Squirrels will bury hickory nuts. Some of the nuts sprout into hickory seedlings and grow into trees.

Mammals possess another quality for man — an aesthetic one. People who like the out-of-doors get enjoyment from catching glimpses of wild mammals and knowing that wildlife exists.

All of these values are worth considering in a conservation approach directed toward the perpetuation or continuation of mammals. Preservation or management plans are needed by man to see that animals do not become extinct, and that they are not ravaged by diseases when they have their own "population explosions."

Mammal

For some odd reason, the word "animal," in most people's everyday language, is used only when speaking of mammals. The bird, the fish, the snake, the toad, and even man have as much right to be called animal as the squirrel or deer. Mammals are the most intelligent of all groups of animals. Compared to the sizes of their bodies, the brains of mammals are larger than those of any other animal group.

Mammals vary greatly in size. The blue whale — the largest animal that has ever lived in water — is a mammal. This whale weighs fifty times as much as an elephant, the next largest living mammal. Another mammal, the tiny shrew, weighs only a few ounces.

Some Characteristics of Mammals

Mammals differ from fish, amphibians, and reptiles, which are known as cold-blooded animals. Mammals and birds are warm-blooded animals, which means they always have a uniform body temperature. Their body stays at normal temperature even when the surrounding air temperature changes.

Mammals have the most highly developed bodies of all animals. The bodies of most mammals are covered at least partly with hair. Two main types of hair make up the coat or pelage. The underhairs, or fur, are thick and soft and lie next to the skin. The guard hairs are fairly long and coarse and lie over the underhairs. However, not all mammals have both types of hair.

One of the most important functions of hair is insulation to help keep the mammal warm. Air is trapped and held within the covering of hair. The hair prevents body heat from being lost and cold air from seeping in.

Hair is the outgrowth of the skin. People who have cats or dogs sometimes find hairs on furniture or their clothes. The mammal is molting. These individual hairs the mammal has lost will be replaced by new ones. In the fur-trade language, a mammal's coat is "prime," or in the best condition, when a new winter coat is complete.

Live Birth

The young of most mammals are born alive. After birth young mammals breathe by means of lungs. Almost all mammals look much like their parents when they are born. The adult mammals usually take care of their young until the young can take care of themselves. The mother mammal nurses her young with milk from her own body.

Limbs

Mammals typically have four legs, or limbs, with toes or digits. They also have nails, claws, or hoofs.

Feet tell what the mammal's habits are with respect to food getting, home building, and their ability to escape their enemies. The feet also leave a record of the mammal — tracks in the dust, snow, sand, or mud.

Otters, muskrats, and beavers are mammals that live part of their lives in water. Their hind feet are webbed for swimming.

Bats, the only mammal capable of sustained flights, have front limbs modified into wings.

Teeth

Many mammals have two sets of teeth similar to ours: milk teeth, which are lost, and permanent teeth. The four general types of teeth occur in order from front to rear of each jaw: incisors, canine, premolars, and molars. Some teeth, such as the incisors of rodents, rabbits, hares, and beavers, continue to grow throughout life.

Rabbits and rodents that clip and gnaw stems have chisel-shaped incisors. These are separated from the cheek teeth by a wide space. The cheek teeth are generally flattened and low-crowned and are well suited for grinding food. Plant-eating animals are called *herbivores*. Meat-eating mammals are called *carnivores*. They have large, sharp canine teeth. These are for piercing and tearing flesh.

Tails

Tails have many uses. A mammal may have several different uses for its tail. A mammal that jumps often uses it for balance. Squirrels use their tails as a sort of blanket. The fox wraps himself up in his tail to keep his nose warm. Tails are often used as danger signals. The whitetailed deer raises its tail in alarm like a white flag.

Beavers slap the water with their tails to help them do a quick dive when danger threatens. The sound made by the slap of the beaver's tail warns other beavers of possible danger. They also use their tails for steering and as an oar to push them through the water. The skunk gives a warning with his striped tail before squirting his scent in times of danger. The porcupine uses its tail as a hammer, driving sharp quills into an enemy which dares to attack.

Vision

We humans, along with the monkeys, have frontal eyes. We need this "binocular vision" (the image seen with one eye overlaps the image perceived by the other) for judging depth and perspective as we walk, drive, or fly about our mechanical environment. Monocular vision is the area seen through one eye.

In all animals, eye position is related to feeding habits, among other things. An animal which hunts other animals is aided by frontal vision. It needs to see what it is chasing and needs the accuracy of binocular vision for attacking its prey.

Carnivores rely on frontal vision for hunting ability. Vegetarians, or vegetable-eating animals, rely on side vision for fleeing ability. The rabbit's blind area of its eye is very much smaller than that of the fox. The area of binocular vision in the rabbit is also much smaller. A rabbit needs vision all around him while he is feeding so that he can see an approaching enemy.

Vision is related, first, to the safety of the animal; second, to its food requirements; and third, to its urge to mate. The degree of vision each animal has is related to requirements, its way of life, and its environment. Ani-

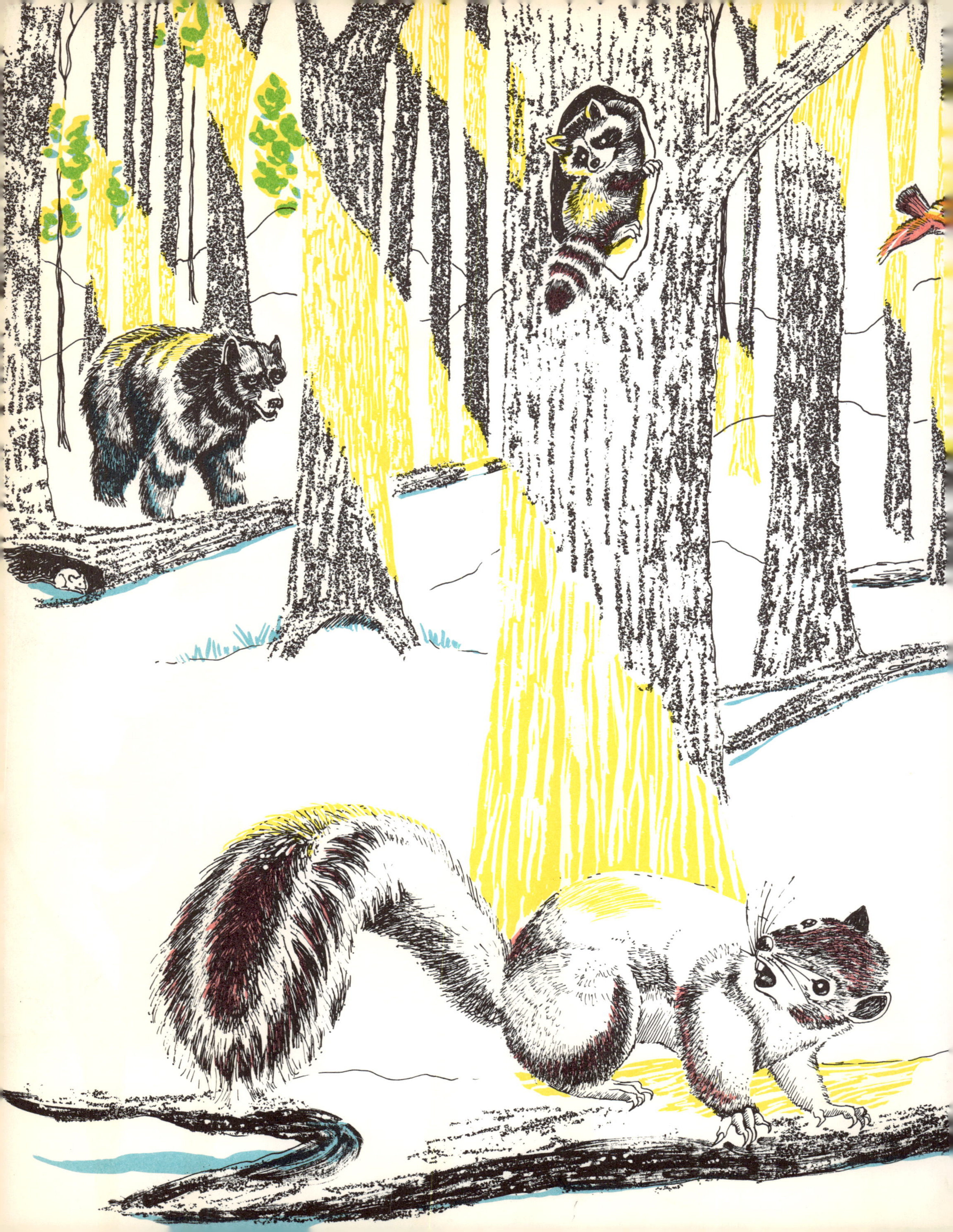

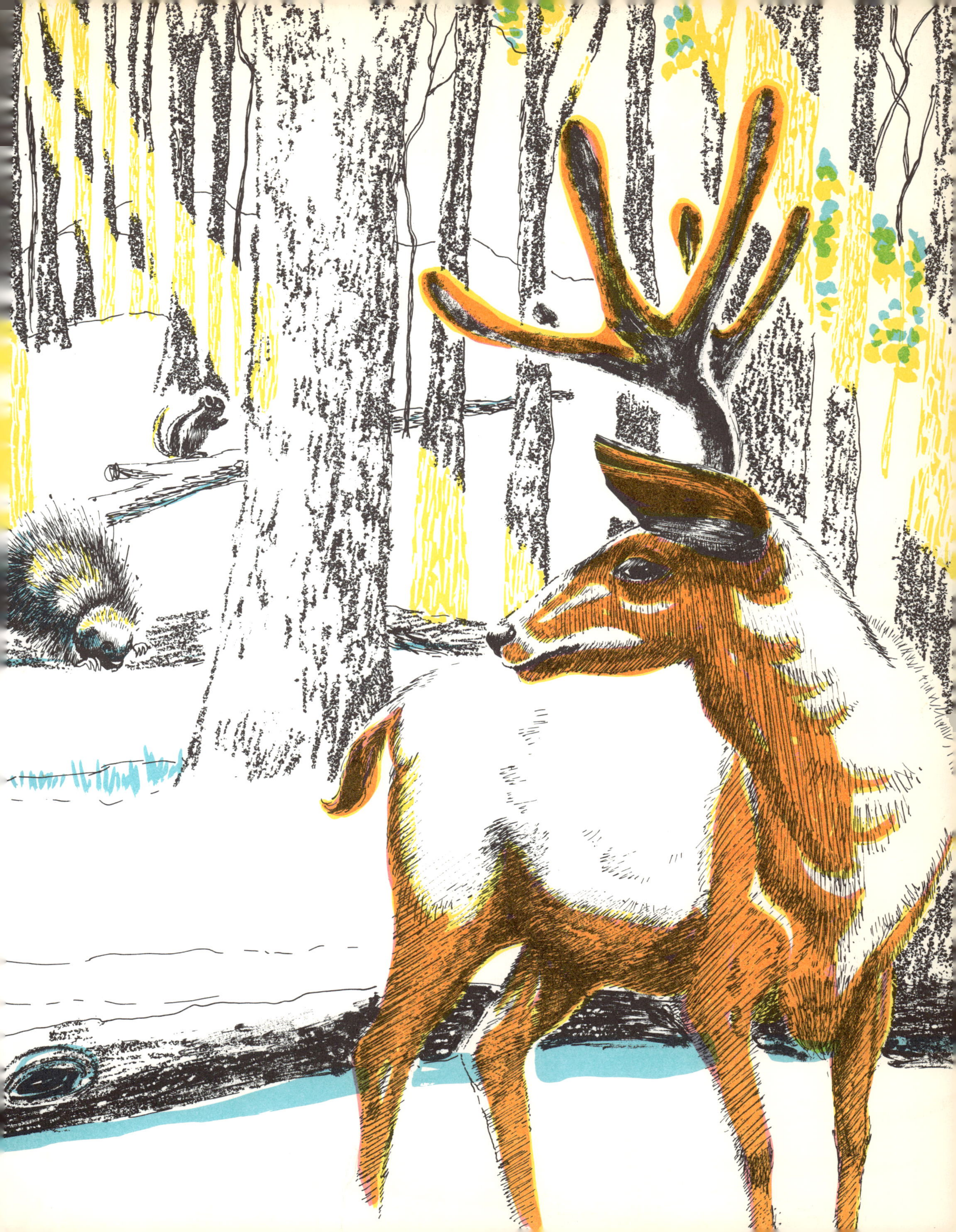

mals which do not see very well have increased abilities to smell or hear, or they are protected by their color.

All mammals, with the exception of the group called the primates, which includes the monkeys and mankind, are more or less color-blind and see nature more in black and white than in color.

Hoofs, Claws, and Toenails

Different kinds of toenails help each animal to live in his own way. Many mammals have big, strong toenails. Deer have very heavy toenails that are thick and almost as hard as stone. Their toenails are called hoofs.

All claws and toenails and hoofs are a sort of hard, dead skin. They aren't really the same as dead skin, but almost. Dead skin doesn't have any feeling in it, and that's why it doesn't hurt to cut off the tip ends of your toenails. And for animals, it's the same way. But if you cut off too much toenail, then it hurts, and it's the same way with animals.

Animals use their toenails for fighting or digging or for holding on to tree limbs. Claws and hoofs and toenails help animals catch food or run or fight or climb trees. Deer stand up on their toenails when they walk. That way they run fast, and the hard ground doesn't hurt their feet. Dogs use their toenails for digging. Cats use their claws in a very special way for catching their food. All cats keep their claws in special little holders made of skin called sheaths, and they are placed right on top of the cat's toes. Cats keep their claws in these sheaths; that way the points don't get dull from walking on rough ground. When cats want to, they can push these claws right out of their holders like sharp little hooks. They use these sharp hooks to catch mice or insects.

Toenails help each animal in a different way. If you see an animal with sharp, curved claws, you can guess that it probably eats meat. But if you see an animal with hoofs, you can guess it eats only plants.

Wild Vertebrates of Farm and Field Land

Approximately 50 percent of the total land area of the United States is farms. Around 40 percent of farmland is classed as cropland, 40 percent as pasture, 15 percent as woodland, and 5 percent miscellaneous. Large numbers of wild animals live upon these lands.

A lad with his first .22 rifle anxiously awaits a trip to a farm in hopes of getting his first cottontail. Rabbits, more than most mammals, have adapted themselves to civilized conditions. The clearing of land has made a better home for them. The cottontail eats many different plants. It does prefer clover, grasses, and grains. In winter it takes whatever it can get, usually bark and buds of green shoots which stick up through the snow.

When chased by an enemy, a rabbit depends on speed and ability to dodge. A cottontail can go faster uphill than down, owing to the greater length of its hind legs. Its long legs enable it to run by swift long leaps, and its long ears give it warning of the approach of danger.

Six other important game species (animals that may be hunted) commonly found in farm habitats in the Eastern and Central United States are ringnecked pheasant, bobwhite quail, Hungarian partridge, gray squirrel, fox squirrel, and woodchuck. All these animals prefer a variety of cover in search of food and shelter. Squirrels may have a permanent home in an oak tree in the farm woodlot and make forays out into nearby grain and cornfields for food. The squirrel's legs are

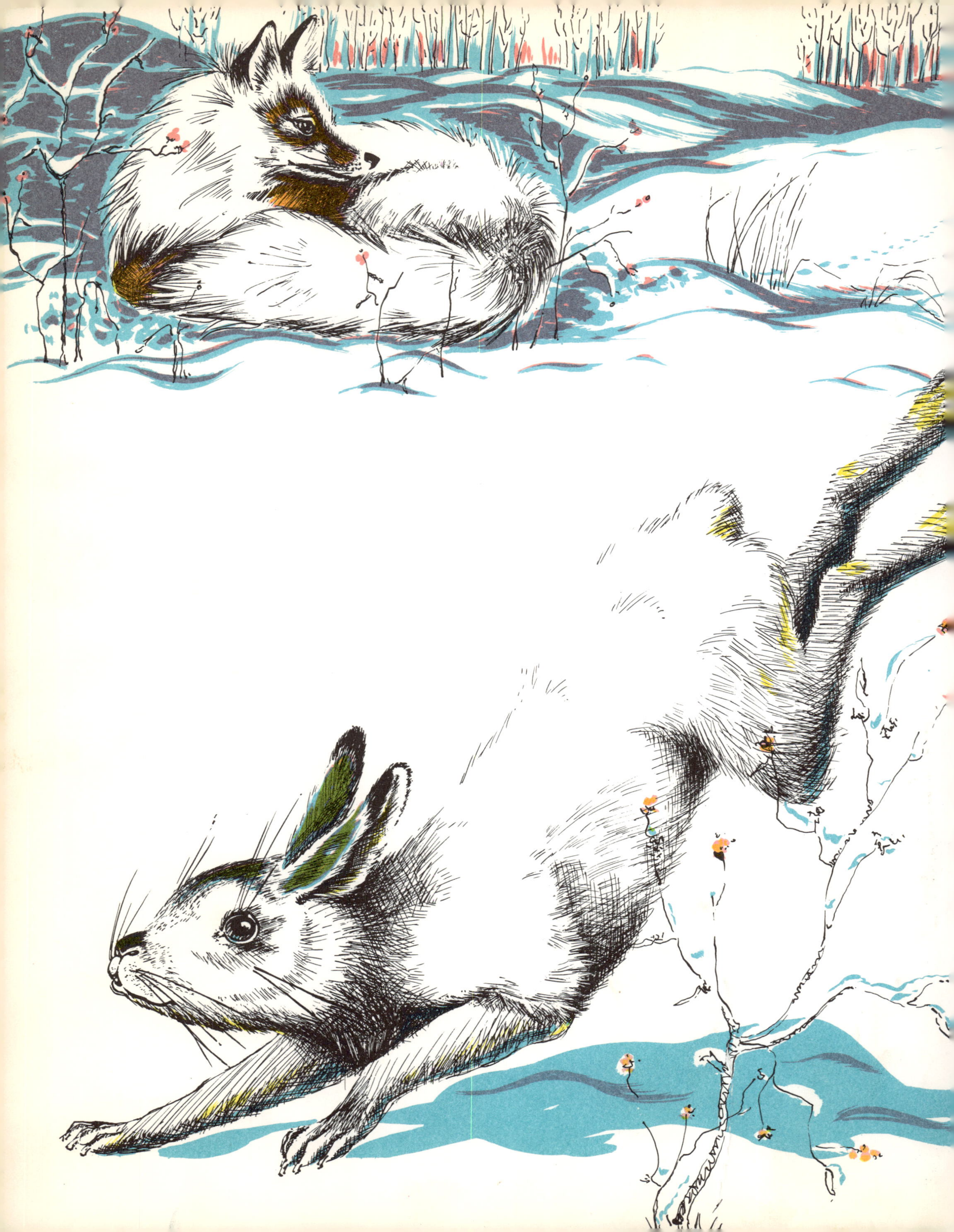

short, and it is more of a climber than a runner. Its strong hips give it power to jump. Squirrels store food for winter in all sorts of places and often forget where they put it. The squirrels may be classed as one of our best planters of nut trees in woodlots.

Most wild animals like hayfields. Food and cover are plentiful and develop early in the season. Hayfields furnish roosting and nesting areas for birds. Another attractive habitat site is grainfields. Both fall- and spring-grown grains supply food of high quality. Cornfields provide excellent cover. Stalks left standing during winter furnish protection for animals that come to feed on waste grain.

Root crops and gardens supply insects for birds and food for rabbits and woodchucks.

The farm woodlot, summer or winter, provides food and cover in one form or another. Gaily colored little chipmunks as well as the ruffed grouse and the flicker are at home in farm woodlots.

The opossum is the only native North American marsupial. The female has a frontal pouch for carrying and nursing its young. They are living fossils or prehistoric survivors. There have been tremendous changes in the earth's surface, climate, and the advancement of civilization. Perhaps the opossum has survived because it eats almost anything dead or alive. The opossum's favorite den site is an old woodchuck burrow. Woodchucks are large rodents that thrive in a farmlot habitat.

The sly red fox helps the farmer by destroying many pests, largely field mice.

Coveys of bobwhite quail are welcomed by farmers. They eat incredible numbers of harmful insects.

Another welcomed bird is the mourning dove with its

mournful "cooing" call. This bird eats an enormous amount of weed seeds.

On Midwest farms the prairie chicken will establish "booming grounds" where it courts a mate by strutting and uttering loud "booms."

Hawks are seen about open fields and hedgerows of farm country. They are beneficial to farmers in destroying field mice that eat valuable crops.

The horned, barn screech, barred, and Richardson's owls are also great destroyers of rats and mice.

Woodpeckers that live in farm areas are helpful because they destroy injurious insects.

Other birds that like a farm habitat are the meadowlark, bobolink, kingbird, red-winged blackbird, Baltimore oriole, purple grackle, cardinal, goldfinch, towhee, sparrows, cowbird, catbird, bluebird, purple martin, barn swallow, starling, and crow.

Vertebrates of the Forest and Wilderness

The virgin forests that covered nearly half of the United States provided homes for vast numbers of animals. Extensive flocks of passenger pigeons may have consumed between 8,000,000 and 9,000,000 bushels of food a day, probably chestnuts and acorns. Today they are extinct. The wild turkey was found wherever oaks and chestnut trees grew. In the original forests, bison, deer, elk, moose, beaver, squirrels, and hares made their homes.

The clearing of forests and drainage of swamps during the 1800s and 1900s reduced the number of animals. Some animals could not adjust to habitat changes; others were

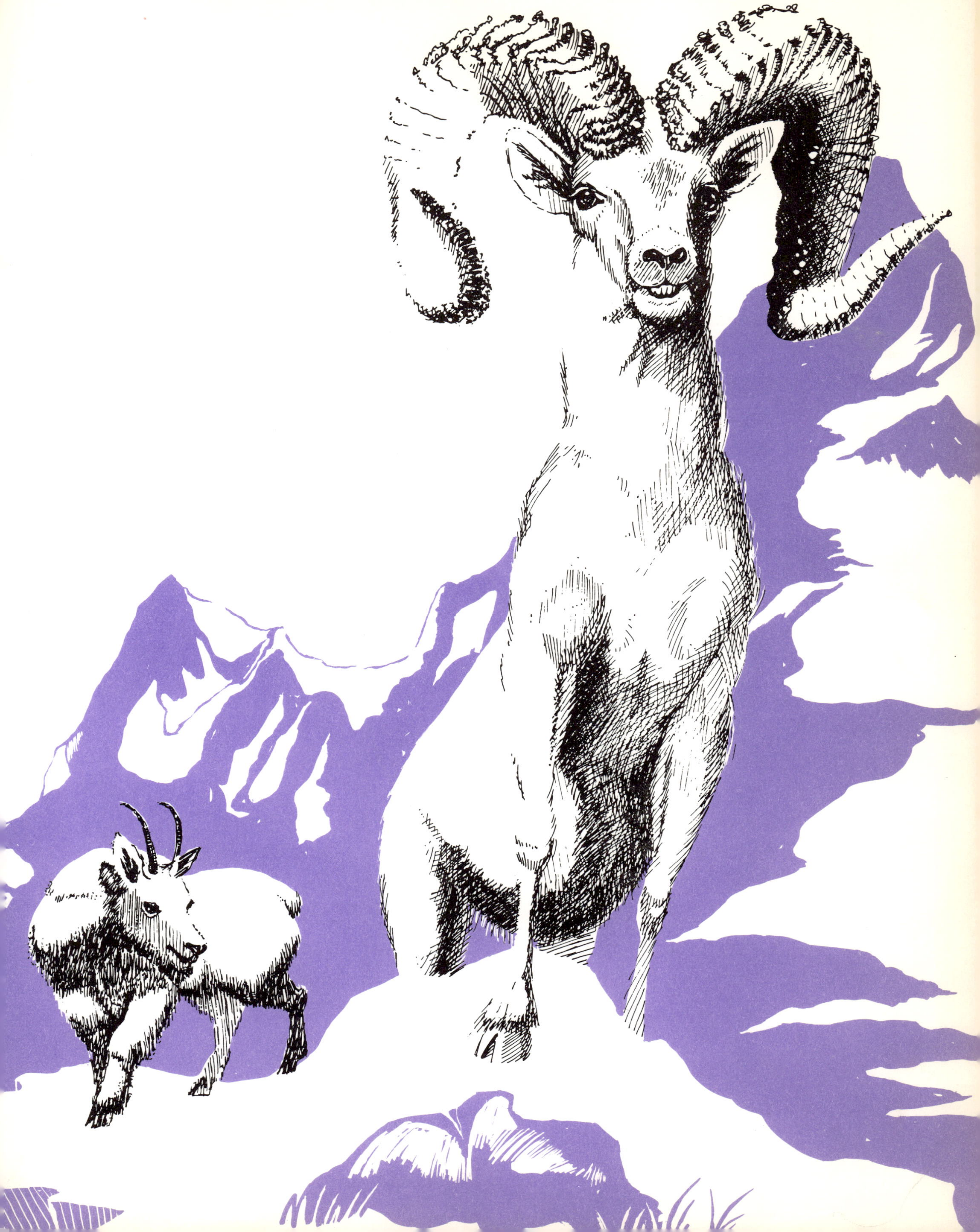

able to survive. Over the last fifty years effective law enforcement and environmental changes have enabled deer and beaver to make a comeback. Their present populations are higher than they have ever been since man came to America.

Only a few wolves remain in the United States. Wolves have been shot, trapped, and poisoned by man. They are safe only in remote forested areas.

Grizzly bears that once roamed the entire West have been pushed into remote areas in the northern Rocky Mountains. They weigh between 600 and 800 pounds. They will eat almost anything — plant or animal. The grizzly bear is now on the critical list of becoming extinct.

Black bears may be found throughout the country in remote forests. Around national parks the black bear may become a nuisance and danger to visitors.

The mountain lion, puma, or cougar prefers rocky, craggy cliffs. They depend on deer, squirrels, rabbits, porcupines, gophers, and rats for food.

The lynx and bobcat are closely related. Both are short-tailed and chunky in build. They live in forested areas.

Three members of the weasel family, the wolverine, fisher, and marten, stay close to the forest. Wolverines demand wilderness; most are found in Alaska. The marten lives in trees. Prized for its rich brown fur, it is heavily trapped. The fisher is almost extinct in the United States.

Mountain goat hoofs are especially adapted for climbing and jumping on steep mountain slopes. Mountain goats are not very numerous. They have long white hair and jet-black horns.

Bighorn sheep inhabit lofty peaks. Thick curling horns of the ram make this animal one of the most prized trophies.

Elk, or wapiti, are much larger than deer. Bulls may have 60-inch-wide antlers and may weigh 700 pounds. Unless harvested by hunters in proper numbers, elk can eat away their winter range and destroy the homes of other wildlife.

Moose need wet meadows where water plants, willows, alder, and other preferred foods are available. These huge shovel-antlered animals may stand around six feet tall.

The porcupine and the woodchuck, or groundhog, live in or near forests. The marmot is found in Western forests. Also found in forests is the snowshoe rabbit or varying hare. Unlike rabbit's hair, their pelts turn white in winter and their young are born with hair and with eyes open. (Jackrabbits are hares. Cottontails are rabbits.)

The common squirrel of the forest is the red squirrel. When camping in the forest, you may be welcomed by the little chipmunk.

The beaver is a valuable forest dweller. Its dam holds backwater needed during dry spells. Beavers create homes for fish and waterfowl and provide an area where desirable plants can thrive. Beaver fur is beautiful and among the most durable of all furs.

In cold, clear forest streams live trout and smallmouth bass. Snakes of the forest include the poisonous timber rattlesnake and the copperhead as well as many harmful and beneficial species.

Birds

Wild turkey requirements are usually pines or dense

stands of other conifers for roosting sites and oak trees for a reliable food supply of acorns.

Both the bald and golden eagle nest in forests. Wildlife scientists have recently concluded that DDT in fish eaten by mother eagles is making eggshells too fragile to protect the babies within. Soon our national bird may become extinct.

Many birds are seen in the forests, such as jays, magpies, grouse, ptarmigan, hawks, woodpeckers, sapsuckers, wrens, thrashers, thrushes, nuthatches, creepers, orioles, warblers, grosbeaks, finches, sparrows, juncoes, and crossbills.

Vertebrates of Marshes, Lakes, Ponds, and Streams

Drainage engineers, agricultural planners, and land promoters sometimes look upon marshes for future developments. These lands have a high value in their present condition as homes for many wild animals.

Mammals found near freshwater are mice, rats, shrews, moles, beavers, raccoons, mink, muskrats, and otters, to name only a few.

The beaver is our largest rodent. Beavers are nature's engineers. They build a dam of sticks and mud. These dams create ponds. Beavers are *herbivorous* animals.

For much of its food, the raccoon depends largely upon animals found in freshwater. Raccoons are *omnivorous*. They eat both animal and vegetable life.

Mink build dens in banks of streams and lakes. Mink are very good swimmers. They are *carnivorous*. Women highly prize the mink made into coats and stoles.

The muskrat's dome-shaped homes built of mud and reeds are often observed in streams and lakes. These animals are vegetable-eating furbearers.

Otters are fun-loving, playful mammals that can swim faster than fish, their principal food.

Birds

Many species of birds are found near freshwater. The mournful cry of the loon on a dark night is awesome. Adult loons have a black-and-white checkerboard pattern of feathers.

Grebes look like small ducks. Unlike ducks, they have small bills. Grebes will dive to elude their enemies.

The white pelican is one of our most interesting birds. It has a large pouch beneath its bill in which it carries food for its young.

The bittern is difficult to observe. When sensing danger, it will stand perfectly still in tall marsh vegetation. With its bill pointed skyward, its long neck with vertical stripes of brown and white feathers blends in with the surrounding foliage.

Swans have necks often longer than their bodies. They are large white birds. Water plants are one of their favorite foods. The trumpeter swan is the largest species of American waterfowl. The trumpeter swan has been given protection by law for years, but today there is much concern over its future.

There are many species of migratory (those which move about with the seasons) geese. They frequent freshwater areas where they get food below the water. Geese are game species, which means that certain times during the year they may be hunted. Wild geese mate for life. Their young are hatched in Arctic waters. Geese and ducks are both known as migratory waterfowl because of their seasonal migration from north to south and back to the north to mate and nest.

Dabbler ducks feed on the surface of water. Some of our better known ones are the mallard, pintail, gadwall, teal, and shoveler. One of the most beautiful American ducks is the wood duck.

Ducks that feed on vegetation below the water's surface are called divers. Some of our divers are the scaup, canvasback, redhead, and ruddy duck.

Mergansers are fish-eating ducks.

It is feared that the handsome white whooping crane

with its carmine-colored head patch and black wing tips may soon become extinct. This bird stands almost as tall as a five-foot man. They feed upon both animal and vegetable life. Whoopers produce only one egg a year.

Sandhill cranes have a slate-gray plumage.

Soots, called mudhens, are quite common. They are black with a white bill.

The killdeer, a member of the plover family, is a small shorebird. They nest on the ground. The babies represent in color the pebbles where they are hatched. This blending with their surroundings is referred to as *protective coloration.*

The woodcock love damp thickets. They have an extremely long tweezerlike bill which enables them to probe and pull earthworms out of the soil.

Yellowlegs are members of the sandpiper family. They are watch guards, and when danger appears, they spring into the air uttering a shrill cry as a warning to other shorebirds.

Gulls gliding on their long wings may be seen almost anywhere near fresh or salt water. Where gulls are found, terns are seldom far away.

The osprey, called fish hawk by some people, is found near larger bodies of both fresh and salt water.

Many insect-eating species of songbirds are found near marshes, lakes, and streams. Some of these are the red-winged and yellow-headed blackbird, warblers, swallows, flycatchers, and wrens.

Amphibians

Frogs, toads, and salamanders are found in freshwater areas.

Reptiles

Turtles and several species of snakes are found near water.

Fish

Water where fish can live must be free of silt, pollution, and poisons. In water where fish cannot obtain sufficient oxygen and food, they die.

Predator fish, such as the northern pike, feed almost entirely on other fish.

Trout can live only in water 68 degrees Fahrenheit or colder.

Fish that live in warmer fresh water are numerous. The more common are carp, perch, bullheads, largemouth and smallmouth bass, crappies, and sunfish. The number of fish in a body of water depends on natural fertility.

Vertebrates Found in Rangeland

Rangeland applies to land with a grass cover. These lands usually have trees and shrubs along watercourses.

The pronghorn antelope is a true rangeland animal. It can run over 40 miles an hour to escape its enemies. Sagebrush is an important food for this mammal.

The badger has a masked face. Its large claws enable it to dig underground for its food supply of prairie dogs, squirrels, pocket gophers, and mice.

Prairie dogs live in colonies called prairie dog towns.

It is estimated that 30,000,000 to 75,000,000 buffalo once roamed the West. They were killed by the hundreds until they were nearly extinct. They became protected by law, and today a few thousand are confined on wildlife refuges in Montana, Oklahoma, and South Dakota.

The jackrabbit may weigh up to eight pounds. It eats the same plants that deer and livestock depend on for food.

The cottontail rabbit lives throughout the United States but is seen in greater numbers in rangeland and farmland habitats. This rabbit is hunted by more sportsmen than any other game animal.

The weasel is a vicious predator and is quite fierce for its size. It eats rabbits, mice, squirrels, birds and eggs, snakes, frogs, and fish. The weasel's reddish-brown coat turns white in winter. When white, weasels are often called ermine.

Mice, rats, and voles are probably the most abundant small rodents in the United States. Many are found on rangeland. They are food for many other animals, such as weasels, foxes, badgers, and coyotes.

Bird life is plentiful on Western rangelands. Sharp-tailed grouse, prairie chicken, sage grouse, magpie, crow, raven, meadowlark, sparrow, hawk, and owl are well fitted to life on the range.

A foreign bird that has been brought to the United States and has been able to adjust to a rangeland habitat and multiply is the Hungarian partridge.

Vertebrates Found in the Desert

The kit fox is a desert dweller and lives mainly on mice and small rodents. The collared peccary, or jabalina, is a wild pig found in Arizona and New Mexico. The prickly pear cacti seems to be one of its main foods.

The turkey vulture is valuable because it eats carrion (dead animals). Its remarkable eyesight allows it to spot dead or dying animals for several miles.

Woodpeckers, swifts, swallows, wrens, flycatchers, thrashers, larks, warblers, orioles, and vireos are found on arid lands. Quails, doves, finches, and sparrows, both seed- and fruit-eating birds, can also be found in desert areas.

Rattlesnakes and some of the other snakes like a desert habitat.

Vertebrates of Coastal Waters

There is far greater number of animal life beneath the surface of the oceans than exist on their shores. The seashore where sea and land meet has more wild animals than any place on dry land.

Man is constantly changing the coastline by his dredging, draining, filling, and polluting. These actions affect animals' habitats.

The blue whale is the largest living animal in the world. It may reach a length of 100 feet and weigh more than 120 tons. Blue whales are hunted by whalers because they are the largest producers of whale oil and blubber. They breathe air and must come to the surface about once an hour to "blow" or get fresh air.

The fur seal was greatly reduced in number because of its valuable fur. Since 1911 the United States Fish and

Wildlife Service has managed the herds, and they are increasing in numbers. Males, or "bulls," may have a harem of up to 100 "cows," each of which gives birth to a single youngster.

The sea otter is another animal extensively hunted for the great value of its soft pelt. They are now protected and are making a slow comeback in number.

The porpoise may frequently be seen leaping and playing in a harbor near a river that empties into the sea. A porpoise is quite intelligent and can be taught a number of tricks.

The most valuable furbearer, the muskrat, raises several litters of young each year in large reed and mud homes found in marshes along our seacoasts.

There are many birds found in a coastline habitat. They are being hurt by drainage of swamps, use of DDT and other pesticides that are eliminating much of their food supply. Herons, ibis, pelicans, cormorants are found on our coasts.

Seabirds observed in coastal waters are the terns and gulls. Our national bird, the bald eagle, feeds along coasts and bays. This dark brown bird with a white head and tail feathers weighs more than 14 pounds and has a wing span of over 90 inches. These birds are becoming fewer in number. They are protected by federal law.

Several species of duck frequent coastal waters, such as oldsquaw, scaup, brant, and scoters.

Coastal marsh birds are the rails, gallinules, coots, and plovers.

Other familiar shorebirds include the sandpiper, killdeer, sanderling, and yellowlegs.

Fish

The largest of all fish, the whale shark, averages 20 feet in length; it has been known to reach a length of 60 feet. Unlike the whale shark, which is harmless to man, the hammerhead shark will attack man or anything in water that looks edible.

The largest of the rays, the Pacific manta, known as the devilfish, may reach over 5,000 pounds in weight. Mantas look somewhat like large bats and propel themselves through the water by beating their winglike arms, moving at tremendous speeds.

Saltwater game fish include sailfishes, marlin, swordfish, tuna, mackerel, albacore, salmon, tarpon, dolphin, striped bass, bluefish, sheepshead, mullet, flounder, and shad.

Bibliography

Allen, Durward L., *Our Wildlife Legacy*. New York, Funk and Wagnalls Company, 1954.

Barker, Will, *Familiar Animals of America*. New York, Harper and Brothers Publishers, 1956.

Callison, Charles H., *America's Natural Resources*. New York, The Ronald Press Company, 1957.

Darling, Lois and Louis, *The Science of Life*. New York, The World Publishing Company, 1961.

Dorian, Edith, and Wilson, W. N., *Animals That Made U.S. History*. New York, McGraw-Hill Book Company, 1964.

Lanyon, Wesley E., *Biology of Birds*. New York, The American Museum of Natural History Press, 1963.

Leopold, Aldo, *A Sand County Almanac*. New York, Oxford University Press, 1949.

Palmer, E. Laurence, *Field Book of Natural History*. New York, McGraw-Hill Book Company, 1964.

Palmer, R. S., *The Mammal Guide*. New York, Doubleday, 1954.

Peterson, R. T., *A Field Guide to the Birds*. Boston, Houghton Mifflin, 1947.

Raskin, Edith, *Watchers, Pursuers, and Masqueraders*. New York, McGraw-Hill Book Company, 1964.

Storer, John H., *The Web of Life*. New York, The Devin-Adair Company, 1954.

Trefethen, James B., *Crusade for Wildlife*. The Stackpole Company, Harrisburg, Pa., Boone and Crockett Club, New York, 1961.

Trippensee, Reuben Edwin, *Wildlife Management*, Vol. I and II. New York, McGraw-Hill Book Company, 1964.

Pamphlets

Allen, Dorothy, *Birds and Game Bird Management*, Virginia Commission of Game and Inland Fisheries, Richmond, Virginia, 1962–63.

———, *Fish and Fishing*, Virginia Commission of Game and Inland Fisheries, Richmond, Virginia, 1962.

Michigan Department of Conservation, Lansing, Michigan, 1957.

National Wildlife Federation, Washington, D.C., 1964.

Nature Bulletins. Forest Preserve District of Cook County, Chicago, Illinois, 1950–1969.

Virginia Commission of Game and Inland Fisheries, Richmond, Virginia.

Wisconsin Conservation Department, Madison, Wisconsin, 1961.

Index

Alligators, 25–26
Amphibians, 17 ff.
  of freshwater areas, 55
Anal fin, 13

Bald eagle, 52
Baltimore oriole, 48
Barn screech owl, 48
Barn swallow, 48
Barred owl, 48
Beaver, 51
Birds, 31–36
  beaks, 32, 34
  body, 35
  of coastal areas, 60
  in desert, 58
  feathers, 32
  of forest and wilderness, 51–52
  internal organs, 34
  legs and feet, 35–36
  of marshes, lakes, ponds, and streams, 53–55
  migration, 31
  in rangeland, 58
  tongue, 34
  vision, 36
Bittern, 54
Black bears, 50
Bluebird, 48
Blue whale, 59
Bobolink, 48
Bobwhite quail, 36, 43, 45
Brant, 60
Brown snake, 28
Bullheads, 56
Bull snake, 28

Canvasback duck, 54
Cardinal, 48
Carnivores, 40
Carp, 56
Catbird, 48
Claws, 42–43
Coastal waters, vertebrates found in, 58–61
Collared peccary, 58
Copperhead snake, 28, 30, 51
Coral snakes, 30
Corn snake, 29–30
Cottonmouth snake, 28, 30
Cottontail, 57
Cowbird, 48
Crappies, 56
Creepers, 52
Crocodiles, 25–26
Crop, 34
Crossbills, 52
Crow, 48, 58

Dabbler duck, 54
Desert, vertebrates found in, 58
Dinosaurs, 22
Dorsal fin, 13

Esophagus, 34

Farmland, wild **vertebrates** of, 43–48

Farm woodlot, 45
Field land, wild vertebrates of, 43–48
Finches, 52
Fish, 11–16
  eyes, 14–15
  freshwater, 56
  growth, 16
  habitat, 15–16
  how it breathes, 13–14
  how it swims, 12
  management, 11
  parts of, 12–13
  saltwater, 61
  scales, 15
  sense of smell, 15
Flycatchers, 55
Forest, vertebrates of the, 48–51
Fox squirrel, 43
Frogs, 17–21
  ears, 20
  eggs, 20
  eyes, 20
  food, 20–21
  shape, 19
  skin, 18–19
Furcula (wishbone), 35
Fur seal, 59

Gadwall duck, 54
Game species, 43–44
Garter snake, 28, 29
Gizzard, 34–35
Glass snake, 24
Golden eagle, 52
Goldfinch, 48
Gray squirrel, 43
Grizzly bears, 50
Grosbeaks, 52
Grouse, 52
Guard hair, 38–39

Hammerhead shark, 61
Hawks, 52, 58
Hayfields, 45
Herbivores, 40
Hoofs, 42–43
Horned owl, 48
Hungarian partridge, 43, 58

Jabalina, 58
Jackrabbit, 57
Jays, 52
Juncoes, 52

Killdeer, 55, 60
Kingbird, 48
King snake, 28, 29–30
Kit fox, 58

Lakes, vertebrates of, 52–56
Largemouth bass, 56
Lizards, 24–25

Magpies, 52, 58
Mallard ducks, 54
Mammals, 37 ff.
  characteristics, 38–39

hoofs, claws, and toenails, 42–43
  limbs, 39–40
  live birth, 39
  tails, 40–41
  teeth, 40
  vision, 41–42
Marshes, vertebrates of, 52–56
Meadowlark, 48, 58
Merganser ducks, 34, 54
Migration, of birds, 31
Milk snake, 28
Milk teeth, 40
Molting, in mammals, 39
Mourning dove, 45
Mucus, on fish scales, 15

Northern pike, 56
Nuthatches, 52

Oldsquaw, 60
Orioles, 52
Osprey, 55
Owls, 58

Pacific manta, 61
Passenger pigeons, 48
Pectoral fins, 13
Perch, 56
Permanent teeth, 40
Pintail duck, 54
Ponds, vertebrates of, 52–56
Prairie chicken, 48, 58
Primary feathers, 32
Protective coloration, 55
Pronghorn antelope, 56
Ptarmigan, 52
Purple grackle, 48
Purple martin, 48

Racer snake, 28
Rangeland, vertebrates found in, 56–58
Rat snake, 28
Rattlesnake, 28, 30
Raven, 58
Red fox, 45
Redhead duck, 54
Red squirrel, 51
Red-winged blackbird, 48, 55
Reptiles, 22 ff., 56
Richardson's owl, 48
Ring-necked pheasant, 43
Ringneck snake, 28
Ruddy duck, 54

Sage grouse, 58
Salamanders, 21–22
  eggs, 21
  food, 21–22
  habitat, 21
  shape, 21
Sanderling, 60
Sandhill crane, 55
Sandpiper, 60
Sapsucker, 34, 52
Scaup duck, 54, 60

Scoters, 60
Sea otter, 60
Secondary feathers, 32
Sharp-tailed grouse, 58
Short-horned lizard, 25
Shoveler duck, 54
Smallmouth bass, 51, 56
Snakes, 27–30
Snowshoe rabbit, 51
Sparrows, 48, 52, 58
Spiny lizards, 25
Starling, 48
Streams, vertebrates of, 52–56
Sunfish, 56
Swallows, 55

Teal duck, 54
Thrashers, 52
Thrushes, 52
Timber rattlesnake, 51
Toads, 17–21
  eggs, 20
  eyes, 20
  food, 20–21
  shape, 19
  skin, 18–19
Toenails, 42–43
Towhee, 48
Trout, 51, 56
Trumpeter swan, 54
Turkey vulture, 58
Turtles, 23–24
Tympanum, 20
Tyrannosaurus rex, 22

Underhairs, 38
United States Fish and Wildlife Service, 59–60

Varying hare, 51
Ventral fins, 13
Vertebrates
  of coastal waters, 58–61
  in desert, 58
  of farm and field land, 43–48
  of forest and wilderness, 48–51
  of marshes, lakes, ponds, and streams, 52–56
  in rangeland, 56–58

Warblers, 52, 55
Waterfowl, 31
  flyways, 31
Water snake, 28
Whale shark, 61
White pelican, 54
Whitetailed deer, 40
Whooping crane, 54–55
Wilderness, vertebrates of, 48–51
Woodchuck, 43, 45
Woodcock, 55
Wood duck, 54
Woodpeckers, 48, 52
Wrens, 52, 55

Yellow-headed blackbird, 55
Yellowlegs, 60

The Author

DOROTHY HOLMES ALLEN, a native of Missouri, served in the Women's Reserve of the Marine Corps in World War II before going on to study education at Oregon State College and conservation at the University of Michigan. For six years, she served as education officer for the Virginia Game Commission, and at the present time she holds a position with a federal resource agency. Mrs. Allen has written a number of teaching units, booklets, and articles about nature study and conservation.